WRITTEN BY
MARGARET DUGDALE
MW01620562
Hamish and the Double Bass

Hamish loved going to concerts with his grandma.

Up to the station, onto the train.

Clickerty-clack, clickerty-clack.

Up the steps
and into the city.

Across the bridge
and over the water.

Past the art
gallery, along
by the fountains.

We're here!

One by one the musicians come in.

Violin, viola and the cello too.

The clarinet, the silver flute, the loopy saxophone and the shiny French horn.

And look, there's the percussion: the timpani, xylophone and a big

bass

drum!

As the lights go down an excited hush settles over the hall and the conductor walks to centre stage.

She watches, waiting,
her arms up.

Musicians ready.

Silence ...

And the music begins!

At first it's soft and slow, like gently falling rain, then strong and fast like rolling thunder.

Closing his eyes
Hamish can hear...

a wandering stream and lions roaring.

He can see birds flying
and stars shining.

He feels his heart beating with the
wonder of it all.

Joyfully hopping and dancing his way out of the concert hall,

Hamish sees a sliver of light through a door.

He opens the door a little.

All alone, leaning
against the wall,
looking forlorn is a

big,

elegant

instrument,

its shoulders
almost golden
in the light.

"Who are you?" asks Hamish politely.

"Why do you look so sad, and why are you alone?"

"I'm the Double Bass."

His voice is deep, rich, strong and just a little sad.

"Nobody wants to play me today."

"I'd like to play you," says Hamish, "but I'm not big enough."

"You'll grow," smiles the Double Bass, "and while you're growing you can learn to play some of my smaller friends."

Hamish does.

And his friends do too. They even make up little rhymes about each other:

Elanora and Mai-Lin learn to play the violin.
They play so well their violins sing.

Emalina, with her long lean fingers, learns to play the fine viola.
She loves its calm and throaty tones and plays it when we do our yoga.

Alex on his clarinet sounds wonderful and dreamy,
like ice cream, rich and creamy.

Stellie loves her silver flute,
she likes to practice in her bathing suit.

When Arjun on the trombone starts,
the sound he makes is more like farts.

But once he gets the hang of it
the sound he makes is one big hit!

Maxie on his golden sax has all of us up dancing,
and when CJ blows his shiny horn we leap around like horses prancing.

Hamish learns to play the cello.
He loves its sound, so
strong and mellow.
Freddie and Uma play percussion –
sometimes quiet, often loud,
it's the beat that makes them proud.
Boom!
Bang!
Crash!
Ting!
Wild excitement is
their thing!

They learn the language of music too: those funny squiggles, lines and dots on the page show them how to talk to their instruments and what to play.

They practise lots and lots and soon discover that there is nothing as much fun or as magical as making music together.

Hamish practises every day.

Then one day he notices that he has grown taller than his Dad,

and that's

tall!

Wasting not a single moment Hamish races to his room, changes into his best clothes ...

and takes off up to the station and onto the train.

Up those steps into the city, his now very long legs taking him up them three at a time.

Breathless, Hamish finds that room at the back of the concert hall.

There he is: big, strong, wise and kind, leaning against the wall.

“Now you’re ready” says the Double Bass.

Hamish laughs, “Come on! We’ve got a concert to play!”

There they are: Hamish and his Double Bass with all their friends in the biggest orchestra, on the biggest stage, in the biggest concert hall you ever saw.

The lights go down, the conductor comes in.

That magical hush falls over the audience.

The conductor watches, waiting, her arms up.

Musicians ready. *Silence ...*

And the music begins!

Fast, slow, loud, soft.

Gentle like rain,
strong like thunder;

wandering like a stream;

lions roaring,

birds flying;

stars shining,

hearts beating.

The audience claps
and shouts,

"Hooray!
Hooray!
More!
More!"

Hamish and his friends, excited and oh so happy, stand and bow.

Glancing across to the audience through the lights, Hamish sees her ...

It's Grandma, smiling at him.

First published in Australia in 2022 by Story Telling Books

ABN 60375257780

Author: Margaret Dugdale

Illustrator: Becky Stout

Designed by Rock Sheep Studio Ltd

ISBN: 978-0-6454108-6-0 (hardback)
ISBN: 978-0-6454108-2-2 (paperback)
ISBN: 978-0-6454108-0-8 (ebook)

Printed by Kindle Direct Publishing

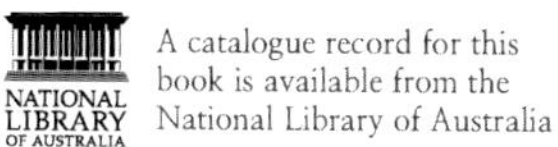

A catalogue record for this book is available from the National Library of Australia

www.storytellingbooks.com

Made in United States
Orlando, FL
08 March 2024